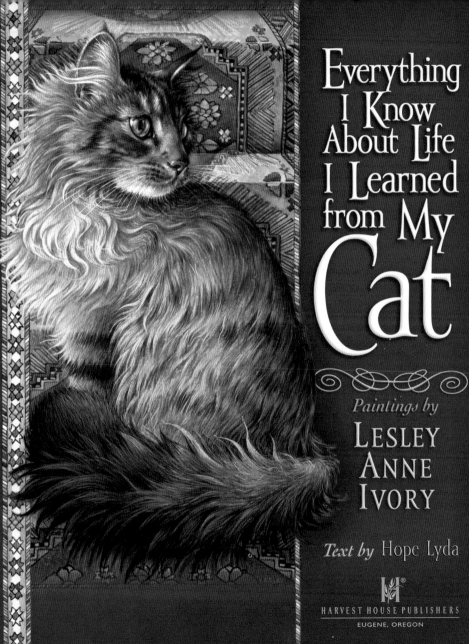

Everything I Know About Life I Learned from My Cat

Paintings by

LESLEY ANNE IVORY

Text by Hope Lyda

HARVEST HOUSE PUBLISHERS

EUGENE, OREGON

Everything I Know About Life I Learned from My Cat
Text copyright © 2006 by Harvest House Publishers
Eugene, Oregon 97402

ISBN-13: 978-0-7369-1521-2
ISBN-10: 0-7369-1521-4

Artwork copyright © Lesley Anne Ivory 2006
Licensed by ⒸOpyrights Group

Design and production by Garborg Design Works, Minneapolis, Minnesota

Printed in Hong Kong

07 08 09 10 11 12 / NG / 7 6 5 4 3 2

Contents

I have studied many philosophers and many cats.
The wisdom of cats is infinitely superior.

Hippolyte-Adolphe Taine

Since each of us is blessed with only one life, why not live it with a cat?

Robert Stearns

The Best Gifts in Life Are Relationships

Perhaps it is because cats do not live by human patterns, do not fit themselves into prescribed behavior, that they are so united to creative people.

Andre Norton

During my first year of marriage, my husband, Marc, and I lived in the suburbs and commuted into the city *together*. This is a challenge I would not recommend to any newlywed. A spouse's differences of opinion, morality, philosophy, and ambition are never quite as blatant as when we trust them at the wheel.

The trickiest part of this commitment was at day's end when I picked up Marc on the corner of a busy intersection. If he wasn't standing there at the time I came by, I would have to drive a wandering city route around the block to try again. In rush hour traffic.

On this particular day, I was keeping a positive attitude because it was Marc's birthday. So when the corner was empty, I did my extra loop and hoped for the best. As I pulled up the second time, he was just exiting the building. Against the wishes of my fellow drivers, I pulled up to the curb and stopped.

A throng of Marc's coworkers peered out the window as

my smiling husband approached our car carrying a white box decorated with a red helium balloon. Inside this box was a small black kitten with pointy ears, a splash of white on his chest, large eyes, and an eager, almost-maniacal grin. I was in love.

Having a spastic kitten might be as daring as commuting with your partner every day; both endeavors involve patience, faith, and well-practiced phrases like "Please stop chewing the carpet" and "Is your shoe made of lead, Honey?"

Both ventures require lots of love. When the patience grows thin and the conversations are strained, when the cat won't stop meowing at night or running laps around the living room, love is the underlying current that keeps life flowing in the right direction.

Any glimpse into the life of an animal quickens our own and makes it so much the larger and better in every way.

John Muir

That birthday-gift cat, Sam, was one of the loveliest cats I have ever known. He was an integral part of my marriage and home life and was my friend and comfort for twelve years.

After Sam had passed away, Marc and I were considering adopting another kitten. A friend's cat had a litter and, on our anniversary, my husband said, "Let's go get our kitty." And so we did. This time, we were much wiser about the care, attention, and humor a small kitten requires. But of course, we also knew that this anniversary decision wasn't about the work. It was about the love we would give and receive. It was about the start of something great. It was about the gift of a relationship...and everything that goes with it.

To this day, Marc can use the free pass of "I brought you the greatest gift on *my* birthday" when he needs grace, which isn't too often...unless, of course, we are carpooling.

6

*A charm of cats is that they seem to live
in a world of their own, just as much as
if it were a real dimension of space.*

Harriet Prescott Spofford

I had avoided getting a pet because of the
commitment involved. Then one day, a cat
came to me. He was tough and a bit of a
loner; I named him Al Capone. In a short time
we were the best of friends. Eventually I added
a kitten to our home, and Al showed the little
one the ropes. One day, Al disappeared and I
was heartbroken. I even hired an animal rescue
professional to come and look for him. Signs
of Al's recent presence were around, but Al
himself was not. Later, I discovered Al was
taken in by a little girl down the road who
was very sick. I realized that Al came
into people's lives when they needed
him most. My time with him was
important, helpful, and he had taught
me how to open my life up to the
commitment and joy of relationships.
JACKIE S.

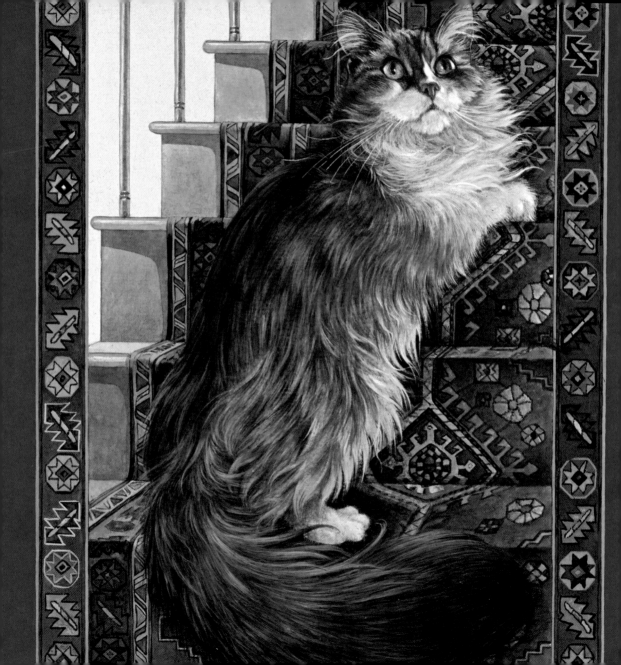

There are few things in life more heartwarming than to be welcomed by a cat.

Tay Hohoff

Never Give Up Hope

Click.

Grind.

Pitter patter. Pitter patter.

Clop. Clop. Clop.

This sounds like the start of a hip-hop song, but it is the symphony in my house which follows the simple act of opening a can. A can of any kind. When I press the teeth of the opener into the flimsy tin holding green beans, corn, beets—the cats come running.

I know what you're thinking. So obvious. The cats assume it is luscious canned cat food being prepped for their *petit dejeuner.* A Pavlov dog's experiment for the smarter species. But my cats are restricted to dry food. The only sound that should delight their perky ears is the tear of a fresh paper bag.

With that first pop of the metal, I believe Katie starts her pitter-patter trot toward the kitchen because she overheard

If a cat did not put a firm paw down now and then, how could his human remain possessed?

Winifred Carriere

wonderful stories about tasty, creamy food from the more experienced cats at the animal shelter. And in turn, Libby's long legs clop because at some point, between face-swatting conditioning and "Knock over that glass bowl...The People like that" lessons that Katie gave Libby...there was one lesson about holding on to the dream. The dream of something better.

It is admirable really—this never-waning sense of hope. Each time they race to the kitchen and I let them sniff at the black beans, they are disappointed, but not so much that they refuse to hold on to the hope of fulfillment.

I consider how many ways I do this same thing. I follow a rabbit trail of aspiration only to dine on disappointment. Yet, in this moment of "not this time" self-condolence, I sense a remaining hope in my heart. A gut-instinct that maybe next time my efforts will work. Or when I am feeling quite positive I get a glimpse of how this labor, this trust, this use of my time and energy is necessary for me to make it to the next step. Not in a "pay my dues" way but in a "build a life" way.

I laugh at my cats and shake my head at their galloping enthusiasm. I will be sad if some day my "Click. Grind," is not followed by "Pitter patter. Clop." Because as futile as it seems, the strides we make toward hope and faith are never without meaning and purpose. Our gangly run might trigger a few snickers from those around us...but in the end, our naiveté is a strength, a virtue. And while some dreams cannot be realized in our lifetime...some can.

After losing my companion Sam (a miniature schnauzer I had for over 15 years), I wasn't sure I was ready for another dog…but I did desire another pet. And along came Piedy, an abandoned cat who was temporarily being cared for by a friend. The first time I met him, he took one look at me and darted under a bed and could not be coaxed out. I couldn't even tell you what he looked like at that point. So I went home without him.

The next day, two others got him out from under the bed using a broom (finally!) and got him over to my place, where he took his second look at me and darted under the printer stand in my home office. And he could *not* be coaxed out. So I let Piedy stay there…for *days*—coming out only after I went to bed. I worried that I had just adopted a mystery pet whose presence would only be known because of an empty food dish and a full litter box. I was losing hope of having the companionship I had with Sam.

After being adored by my dog, this was a little hard to take.

I remember lying on the couch one evening, watching TV, ignoring my doubts about this stray cat's pet potential, when I heard this plaintive little "meow." This little black-and-white head with the prettiest green eyes peered around the couch. That was my moment of love at "first sight." There was my pet, my Piedy. And he was beautiful.

And, it turns out, he is a rather affectionate cat and has become exactly the companion I had hoped for.

First impressions…with people or cats, can leave something to be desired. But when we invest in one another, hope shows its little face.

BARB S.

15

A cat is there when you call her—if she doesn't have anything better to do.

Bill Adler

Personal Space Is Good

Anyone with a cat begins to understand…or at least witness the significance of… personal space. Within moments of being introduced to a new home, cats seek out future favorite nooks, private lounge corners, sun-bathing spots, and prime real estate in your home. It soon becomes clear that the home you chose so carefully had nothing to do with your pleasure but the potential pleasure of your cat.

I have always been a personal space-obsessive being. I scout out places of refuge. The corner table at a coffee shop, the ideal empty aisle at the bookstore, the roomy end seat in a movie theater row. But the cats I have owned over the years (or as many people would wisely say… *the cats who have owned me over the years*) have taught me that my habits are not necessarily those of an antisocial being but are, in fact, normal and good and quite possibly the nature of one who does like others. Just not all the time.

I used to feel guilty about my need for solitary places. It

seemed selfish or distant...even rude when others cohabitated with me. After watching cat after cat shun the public areas of my home and embrace the cozy closet corners, under-the-bed boxes, and hard-to-reach regions of the spare room, I realized that some of us need this kind of time and space in order to restore energy, to explore our deepest or silliest thoughts, and to regain appreciation for others.

Of all animals, he alone attains to the Contemplative Life.

Andrew Lang

It is a spiritual practice even if we are just curling up with a good book, catnapping, journaling, or staring at (and appreciating) the intricate spider web we meant to clean a week ago. These are all exercises in solitude and gratitude in one way or another. And while my cats choose when to bestow affection upon me, I have noticed how grateful and loving they are after having indulged in an afternoon of rest and renewal. Suddenly I am that really neat person who scratches the ideal spot under the chin when just this morning I was the loud, inconsiderate clod who pushed the cats off the bed.

Time alone. Time spent in thought, in reflection, in one's head and heart, makes life a better place filled with better people.

Excuse me, I need a nap.

Dogs come when they're called; cats take a message and get back to you later.

Mary Bly

Be Careful
What You Ask For

There once was a kitty named Nicky. He was gray and white…with an invisible but very evident yellow streak of cowardice down his back. If the doorbell rang, Nicky ran under the couch. He never really connected with anyone in the family; he was too busy running.

Then there was Murphy. He was a big tomcat with wonderful, wise eyes and a good-natured heart. He loved his family and barely tolerated the little pipsqueak named Nicky. While Murphy was confident and smooth, Nicky was scattered. Uncertain. Very unfocused. And more than a little indecisive. In Nicky's goofy misfit world, objectives came and went. Anything could distract him and he never quite thought things through. Sadly, Nicky is a perfect illustration for the wisdom, "Look before you leap."

When the two cats were outside, Nicky, of course, wanted to be inside. Murphy, always the gentleman, was willing to

The Cat was a creature of absolute convictions, and his faith in his deductions never varied.

Mary E. Wilkins Freeman

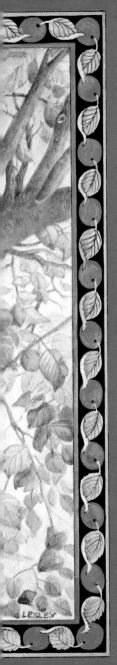

oblige. He would snag the screen door with his claw and let Nicky go first.

The main door, however, was still shut.

We would come home and find Nicky stuck between the doors, crying, confused, and none the wiser. I don't recall, but I suspect Murphy was sleeping nearby waiting for us to see proof of his willingness to accommodate his buddy.

When we are impatient and pulled in a hundred directions, we set ourselves up to make decisions that don't move us forward, but actually keep us stuck. Nicky was sincere, but he could not see past his immediate desire to the consequences that waited between here and there. The fact that we found Nicky in this

Cats seem to go on the principle that it never does any harm to ask for what you want.

Joseph Wood Krutch

compromised position several times only goes to show that even the worst decisions are easy to repeat if we don't stop and take notice.

In my own life, I can look back and see obvious patterns of destruction or at least impairment. They are so clear in hindsight. But while they are happening...while I step through a door merely because I insisted it be opened, I often have missed the open door I was meant to cross through.

As we examine our hopes and dreams, may we always take a moment to consider what awaits us across the threshold...and perhaps *who* is opening the door.

23

There is no snooze button on a cat who wants breakfast.

Author Unknown

Ritual Is Important

Over the years, cats have shown me how to add the tether of ritual to my own day. But mostly, they have reminded me when I become a ritual slacker.

During seasons when life gets too busy, Katie and Libby remind me to play. They model the grace of reckless behavior when I need it most. In my state of rigid control and burden gathering, I covet the way a cat can scoff at too much frivolity in one moment and take an irreverent flying leap in the next. My heart is lighter after watching them tumble across the back of the couch, shimmy down windowsills, repel off the bookshelf, and toss small, plastic balls (real and perceived).

If the desire to sleep in overtakes me, Katie cries with kitty breath in my face or tugs on my hair. Libby is less delicate. She will body slam Marc when breakfast awaits. Through truncated cries that half-acknowledge the early hour, they are telling us

Way down deep, we're all motivated by the same urges. Cats have the courage to live by them.

Jim Davis

Why let the pleasures of life slip us by?
And they are right.

My favorite ritual of all is that which precedes bedtime. Not only because it signals the entrée to sleep, but because it is comforting and nurturing. When ten o'clock is turning to eleven o'clock, Libby starts hanging out near Marc or me. She is a shepherdess taking count of her charge before nightfall. When we put our book down or stir from the computer monitor, she looks at us and slowly closes her eyes like they are weighted with catnip-stuffed mice; it is beyond her physical control to keep them open another minute.

In these days of tension, human beings can learn a great deal about relaxation from watching a cat, who doesn't just lie down when it is time to rest, but pours his body on the floor and rests in every nerve and muscle.

Murray Robinson

If we do not heed this obvious signal, she wanders up and down the hall hoping we will follow her to the bedroom. She is not happy until the nightly devotion has been read, the glow of the bedside lamp is extinguished, and she can climb atop the fabric-covered mountains of slumbering humans and claim her victory: her herd is asleep and she has, once again, brought them safely back to the corral.

Ritual is routine spruced up, elevated to spiritual discipline. Ritual gives a flabby life shape, contours, and content. Ritual feeds us from the inside out and ultimately leads us home.

Through the kitchen window, I was watching Tom, the stray tomcat that had made his home at my father's house. He was flat to the ground doing a military crawl toward a group of birds that were eating fallen seeds below the bird feeder. His heart was willing, and judging from the birds, mice, and moles he had been leaving on the back patio, he was able.

Tom's eyes were wide. His muscle-taut, black coat shone almost blue in the sun. He was no longer Tom, who I pet into a purring fest; he was Tom, the wildcat of ancient jungles. Tom, The Hunter.

Who wants to witness a bird killing? So, I yelled out the open window in the high-pitched, staccato voice I used to call him in from the neighborhood, "Tom-Tom!"

Simultaneously, the birds flew in a scattering of wings and Tom, though remaining in his crouched position, whipped his head to the side and glared right into my eyes as if saying, "Are you nuts? Do you know what I was trying to do?"

About an hour later, the same scenario offered itself. Again I called out "Tom-Tom!" The birds scattered again, but Tom did not move. I didn't see him flinch. I continued calling his name, and he remained poised and ready to complete his task if the birds should ever return. He was determined to maintain the cat ritual of the hunt even if the human was ruining the fun.

KARI V.

Cats are a mysterious kind of folk.
There is more passing in their minds than we are aware of.

Sir Walter Scott

A Life Is as Good as the View

Indoor cat.

The term always evoked images of teary-eyed kittens—little Pinocchio figures who just want to be real cats like the ones they see fighting in the driveway or chasing squirrels.

But when I heard statistics in favor of indoor cats' health versus that of their *au naturel* counterparts, I was willing to give it a try. The fact that we live very close to an increasingly busy main street also cast a vote in favor of safety first.

Thankfully our house has many windows under which I strategically arranged our furniture so they are cat-accessible. On nice days I open up the windows so a breeze blows through the screens and fills Katie and Libby's lungs with the air they need to keep dreaming.

My heart aches a bit when Katie storms the door upon our entrance or exit. She is our little escape artist whose efforts are occasionally rewarded with a few minutes of lawn time.

In a cat's eye, all things belong to cats.

English Proverb

Otherwise, her desire for the outdoors remains on the list of things hoped for.

But the girls are happy. They have excitement and entertainment at every view. What we get from life depends on what we see from where we stand. This is true for me personally. I might want to rush past the doorway of my circumstances to the green grasses of another's life or lifestyle, but when I pay attention to the scene from my existence, many beautiful pieces form the kaleidoscope I call my own. When I am feeling scared, I have the safety and comfort of the life I have been blessed with (complete with responsibilities and obligations). When I want courage, I view the many good life triumphs and experiences in my rearview mirror as well as the promises ahead on the pale pink horizon.

From where I stand today, images of favorite moments, homes, trials, successes, vibrant colors, adventures, communities, friends, and possibilities rush toward me and fill my heart with the breath of life I need to keep dreaming.

There is no more intrepid explorer than a kitten.

Jules Champfleury

When the new job offer came through, I loaded up my two cats in the car and what earthly possessions hadn't been packed into the moving truck and set off to drive across country to start a new life. Several pet-friendly motels and Starbucks later, we arrived on the West Coast.

After the travel-weariness wore off and things were a bit settled, I sat in the middle of my new, empty apartment and cried my eyes out. I cried for the life and friends I had left behind. I cried about the unknown future that lay ahead of me. I cried because I was so tired from all that driving and had to start a new job the next day. I cried because it was my thirty-first birthday and I was all alone except for my two cats. And then one of them, Mo, came and sat on my lap and looked at me like I was crazy. He started to bat at my tears as they fell down my cheeks and that made me laugh. And just for a moment I could hear that still small voice saying, "Keep trusting."

SHANA F.

To understand a cat,
you must realize that
he has his own gifts,
his own viewpoint,
even his own morality.

Lilian Jackson Braun

Cats are absolute individuals, with their own ideas about everything, including the people they own.

John Dingman

Love the One You Are With

Though cats don't admit that they like anything all that much, they definitely have favorites—foods, times of day, nap spots, and people. For example, in my home, Libby likes my husband, Marc, and Katie prefers me.

But cats, with all their other-worldly wisdom, understand what it takes for survival and to get what they want from whomever is around. When I travel and Marc is left alone with both cats for several days, Katie understands whom she needs to love. Marc is her source for food and affection.

After a day, Katie realizes that when Marc sits down to read his book in the evening and drink his tea, he is willing to pet her if she cuddles up next to him on the couch. She

Time spent with cats is never wasted.

Colette

37

Cats love one so much—more than they will allow. But they have so much wisdom they keep it to themselves.

Mary E. Wilkins Freeman

notices that his deep voice with Southern inflections makes for a fine lullaby. When she stands at the back window and watches Marc tend to the yard, she is quite astonished how entertaining he can be. In just a short while, Katie discovers that he is kind, good, and a fine companion for a girl.

When I return from my trip, Katie welcomes me back with glee. Her purrs tell me that Marc just doesn't cut it; I'm the only one for her. But just as I am about to believe her, I see her look longingly at the nook between Marc's arm and the couch pillow. What a comfy nap locale that would be, her eyes seem to say.

Oh, how much alike are we? Before I left for the trip, I had a list of great reasons to be away from Marc for a while. But after my absence, I too see him in a new light. Suddenly, when he sits down to read his book and drink his tea, I want to sit next to him on the couch. His soothing voice steadies my travel-weary mind. And in a short while, I rediscover that he is kind, good, and a fine companion for a girl.

Suspended in a state of limbo, my husband and I plod through each day. The fun leaks from our lives ever so gradually—kids grown and on their own, a house that can't be sold due to a class-action lawsuit over defective siding, the tireless search for a new home, marking time amid a sea of boxes in a tiny rental. The dullness of life that has become familiar lifts slightly when our son moves home after an eight-year stint with the U.S. Navy. We rush to hold him close but in the same moment release him to his own dreams. The adorable calico kitten he brings home is met with little resistance—of course, he will take her with him when he goes! With quiet resolve, tender reassurances, and irresistible treats, we work to win the heart of this skittish ball of fur that holds everyone at paw's length. A year later, our son living miles away with his new bride, my husband and I settle into a new home—with the cat—and taste the sweetness of life once more. We have enticed her to trust and, in return, she has dissolved the intensity that had become our lives and coaxed us to love, laugh, and play again.

NANCY S.

He sits by the window and soaks up the sun,
And curls in my lap when the day is done.
My feline friend, how perfect is he,
His unconditional love...what a blessing to me!

Veronica Curtis

Miracles Can Happen

I was devastated.

My cat, Sam, was missing. We had gone to the beach for a long weekend and when we returned, he was nowhere to be found. My friend Jackie joined me to walk the flat streets behind my house and the hills just beyond the neighborhood to help me look for my runaway. On my morning drive to work, I would slow down or stop if I saw a black cat of any shape or size on somebody else's porch or scurrying into the brush. I began to imagine black cats leaping and running everywhere I went.

I was heartbroken. I called the nearby vet to find out how to best search for a lost cat. They said I could post a note in their office and check with the local humane society. Sam's habit of losing collars meant he had no real identification on him. At best, he might have the tan flea collar I got him a few weeks ago.

One day, in the midst of this grief, I was to meet a friend of mine who lived a couple hours away. Maybe the drive will do me good, I thought. My guilt for leaving town when this was not yet resolved was getting the best of me. I would try

When I'm discouraged, he's empathy incarnate, purring and rubbing to telegraph his dismay...

Catheryn
Jakobson

just one more thing. Before I headed north, I would drive by the vet's office and check their board or ask more questions.

Waiting my turn in a busy office surrounded by yippy dogs and perturbed cats almost sent me out the door. But finally my turn with the harried receptionist arrived, and I meekly explained my unfixable circumstance. Her empathy was comforting, but I could see she was about to explain there was nothing she could do. She paused and asked what color his collar was. I perked up, "Tan...it was light tan." Her disappointment was obvious. She shook her head and said, "Oh, we have an injured black cat brought in this past week but he had a dark collar on. I'm sorry. If you want to go check, we can take you to the back room."

I shook my head. Why would I want to see someone else's hurt cat? I was already an emotional wreck. But as I was about to say "no thanks" I said, "Okay." And I followed the woman to a long narrow room lined with cages.

"Just up here on the left," she said. And as she did, I followed her point with my eyes and noticed that a light tan collar was attached to the outside of the last cage.

The receptionist realized her error and she looked back at me with surprise and hope. I hurried toward the cage saying, "Sammy?" In retrospect I see me running in slow motion like some sappy romance drama from the thirties. Running while holding my hat as my true love is about to leave the train station for Siberia.

Sometimes the wonderful, hard things are comical. Especially when the drama of human emotion repaints the memory. As I approached the cage, I could hear Sam crying. He recognized my voice and was literally throwing himself into the metal door. Through his drug-induced fog, he was trying to reach me.

I opened the cage and held him close. He had been hit by a car at night and

somebody brought him in to the vet's. The doctors had cared for him for several days, but with some stitches and scratches, he was deemed "unadoptable" and was designated for an unhappy fate the next day. (I told you this was like a black-and-white war/love movie.)

I gladly paid the bill to the doctors who were willing to care for a cat without a known owner. I thanked everyone. Cancelled my day trip. And rushed home to play cat-nurse.

There were many moments that day when hearts were tugged in important directions—I stopped at the office on my way out of town; the receptionist mentioned the cat; I walked the narrow corridor thinking it was useless; and the doctors held on to this sad, hurt cat a day longer than usual.

In my eyes, it added up to a miracle.

And I learned to believe that when we follow those gentle God nudges—the ones that bypass logic and reason and go straight to the heart of things—miracles fill our days.

One freezing cold February night, I thought I heard a sound outside the door. When I was about to write it off as my imagination, I heard it again. I got up and looked out the peephole. Nothing. Then I cracked the door open, and there, on our doormat, was a small black-and-white kitten, shivering and mewing pitifully.

I scooped her up and brought her in the living room. She calmed instantly and after a few moments was snuggled in my arms. I noticed she had a collar with a tag dangling from it. Turning the tag carefully, I saw her name and a phone number engraved on it. Her name was Noel. I guessed that she was somebody's special Christmas gift.

I called the number and a woman immediately answered the phone. I told her I had her kitten, and she started to cry. They had just moved into the area, and one of her preschool-age children had left the door open as they were coming into the house. By the time she had noticed Noel's absence, it was night and she couldn't leave her young children to go search. She didn't know what to do.

My roommate and I drove to Noel's nearby home and handed the now warm and playful kitten back to her owner. The very next day I purchased identification tags for my cats. They have never wandered away on a dark winter night, but if they ever do, I hope someone will hear them on their doorstep, help them get warm, and bring them home.

KIM M.

By loving and understanding animals, perhaps we humans shall come to understand each other.

Dr. Louis J. Camuti